In Touch With Nature
Butterflies and Moths

BLACKBIRCH®
PRESS

THOMSON

GALE

San Diego • Detroit • New York • San Francisco • Cleveland • New Haven, Conn. • Waterville, Maine • London • Munich

PHOTOGRAPHIC CREDITS
Art Explosion: 28b, 29br, 30tl; **Image Ideas Inc:** 1, 4–5, 9, 30br; **USDA/ARS:** 5t, 25t, 30tr; **USFWS:** 3, 7, 8, 12–13, 14–15, 18–19, 24–25, 26–27, 28t, 29tl, 29bl, 29tr, 30bl.

Step-by-step photography throughout: Martin Norris

Front cover: Martin Norris and Photodisc

Consultant: Mark Hostetler, Ph.D.,
Assistant Professor, Extension Wildlife Specialist,
Department of Wildlife Ecology & Conservation,
IFAS, University of Florida

For The Brown Reference Group plc
Editorial and Design: John Farndon and Angela Koo
Picture Researcher: Helen Simm
Illustrations: Darren Awuah
Managing Editor: Bridget Giles
Art Director: Dave Goodman
Children's Publisher: Anne O'Daly
Production Director: Alastair Gourlay
Editorial Director: Lindsey Lowe

LIBRARY OF CONGRESS CATALOGING-IN-PUBLICATION DATA

Available from the Library of Congress.

ISBN: 1-4103-0123-0

Printed and bound in Singapore
10 9 8 7 6 5 4 3 2 1

Contents

What are butterflies?

Did you know?
To people with sensitive noses, the wall brown butterfly smells just like chocolate.

Butterflies are colorful insects, with big, triangular wings. On summer days, they flutter slowly from flower to flower to sip nectar. Moths are a similar shape, but they are usually less brightly colored than butterflies. They tend to fly mostly at night.

Butterflies and moths make up a large order (group) of insects called the Lepidoptera.

The Lepidoptera include more than 165,000 different kinds of butterflies and moths. Of these, 145,000 are moths and just 20,000 are butterflies. They live everywhere in the world, except Antarctica. The greatest variety is found in tropical rain forests.

Swallowtail butterfly
This butterfly is seen in the far north of North America and across Europe and Asia.

Did you know?
The smallest butterfly in the world is the dwarf blue of Africa. It is just 0.6 inches (1.4 cm) across.

CLOSE-UP *Moths versus butterflies*

Butterflies and moths are very similar, but there are some differences. Butterflies usually have brightly colored wings and fly only in the daytime. They have slim bodies without much hair. Their antennae, or feelers, are shaped like clubs, with a knob at the end. Moths, however, are usually much duller colored—though there are some striking exceptions. They fly mainly at night, and rest on tree trunks or leaf litter by day. Moths also tend to have fatter bodies covered in thick hair. Their antennae are feathery or threadlike. When resting, a butterfly folds its wings up flat. A resting moth spreads its wings back like a tent, so that only the upper sides are visible.

Moths typically have drab wings. They also spread their wings flat, like this, when resting.

Butterflies vary widely in size, shape, and color. In North America, the smallest is the pygmy blue, which is tinier than a thumbtack. Monarchs have wings more than 4 inches (10 cm) across. The biggest butterfly in the world is the rare Queen Alexandra's birdwing of Papua New Guinea. The female has wings more than 11 inches (28 cm) across.

Moths are even more varied in size than butterflies. The smallest have wings less than 0.1 inches (3 mm) across. American moon moths or luna moths have wings 12 inches (32 cm) across. The wing shapes of moths are also varied.

Like many insects, butterflies and moths look totally different at each stage of their lives. Butterflies and moths begin life as eggs. When they hatch they look nothing like their adult selves. Instead, they emerge as long worm-shaped creatures with many legs. These worm-shaped creatures are called caterpillars. All insects change throughout their lives, but only butterflies and moths begin life as caterpillars.

Butterfly bodies

The best way to learn about butterflies and moths is simply to watch them. You can see them in your yard, or in woods or fields. Moths are hard to spot because they rest during the day. Their drab colors hide them well in their resting places, so you have to look closely to find moths. Butterflies fly by day and are much easier to see.

To get a closer look at butterflies, you may collect them alive and then set them free again. If you do collect butterflies, remember they are living creatures, so treat them gently. This project shows you how to make a net for catching butterflies in the air. It is much more lightweight than an insect sweep net so as not to damage the butterflies' delicate wings.

MAKING A BUTTERFLY NET

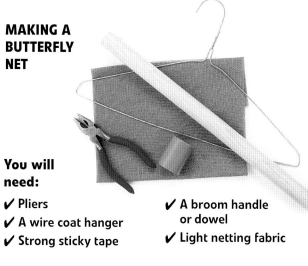

You will need:
✔ Pliers
✔ A wire coat hanger
✔ Strong sticky tape
✔ A broom handle or dowel
✔ Light netting fabric

Did you know?
The front and rear wings of moths are separate, but they act as one because they are hooked together.

1 With an adult's help, use a pair of pliers to open up the wire coat hanger and bend it into a hoop about 10 inches (25 cm) across. Leave the ends straight for fitting the net handle later.

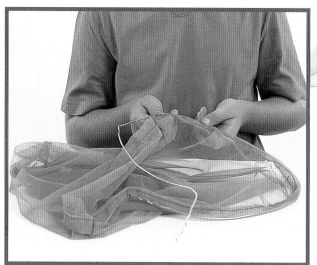

2 Ask an adult to make a triangular bag by sewing together the edges of a triangular piece of the netting. Leave a wide hem at the open end. Feed the wire hoop through the hem.

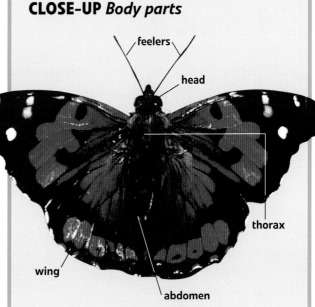

CLOSE-UP *Body parts*

feelers

head

thorax

wing

abdomen

3 Bend the two straight ends of the hoop together and lay them on top of the broom handle or dowel rod. Now wrap tape around and around the handle and the wire to attach the net to the handle.

Look closely at a butterfly. You will see that, like all insects, it has a body divided into three parts. These are the head, the thorax, and the abdomen. The head is where the butterfly's mouth, eyes, and feelers (antennae) are. The thorax is the fat middle section. This contains the main muscles that power the wings and legs. The abdomen is the tapering rear section. This is where the butterfly digests food. Like all insects, butterflies and moths have no bones. But their body is encased in a hard shell, or exoskeleton. This is often covered in hair. Unlike other insects, though, butterflies and moths also have their own unique features. These include their big, flat wings, and their long tongue, or proboscis.

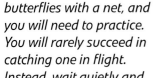

Catching butterflies

It is not easy to catch butterflies with a net, and you will need to practice. You will rarely succeed in catching one in flight. Instead, wait quietly and patiently until it settles on a flower. Then swing your net quickly but very gently. Then hold the net closed to trap the butterfly. Let it go when you have finished looking at it.

Did you know?

When butterflies rest, they fold their wings upward together. Moths lay theirs flat.

Fluttering wings

Did you know?
Fast-flying hawkmoths have wings that are flat and angled back like the wings of a jet plane.

Butterflies and moths get their scientific name from the tiny scales that cover their wings. The word Lepidoptera comes from two ancient Greek words: *lepis*, meaning "scales," and *pteron*, meaning "wings." The scales are so delicate they can rub off like dust if a butterfly is handled carelessly by humans.

The scales on a butterfly's wings are flat, just like tiles. It is these tiny flat scales that give the wings their color. Underneath the scales, a butterfly's or moth's wings are clear like any other insect's. Each of the scales is a different color, so the colorful patterns on a butterfly's wings are built up just like a mosaic.

The wings are supported on a network of fine veins. The veins are filled not just with blood, but also with nerve fibers and air. The flat spaces between the veins are called cells.

How butterflies fly

Butterflies and moths fly in a different way than other insects. Most insects beat their wings very fast to stay up, and soon run out of energy. Butterflies and moths have big enough wings to use the air itself to bear their weight, like a parachute.

Many butterflies ripple their wings slowly up and down to fly. Others, like white admirals, can glide along on air currents.

CLOSE-UP *Wing colors*

Usually wing scales get their color from colored chemicals, or pigments. In some butterflies, however, the color comes from the way that the structure of the scales reflects light. As light is reflected from these scales, it separates into bright, shimmering colors that seem to change as the wing moves. This is called iridescence. It gives the brilliant blues, purples, and greens you can see on butterflies such as the blue morpho of Brazil.

The bright orange of a monarch butterfly's wings comes from chemical pigments in the scales on its wings.

Giant wings

Big wings give extra support, so a butterfly, like this mourning cloak, can fly farther than other insects.

Just an occasional flutter is enough to keep them up. This means they can fly huge distances. Monarch butterflies are known to fly across the Atlantic Ocean, for instance.

Twisting wings

To the human eye, it looks as if a butterfly's wings simply flap. But special photography shows that they actually bend and twist as they move up and down. The bending and twisting pushes air backward and drives the butterfly forward. The wings are stiff around the edge. The stiff front edges help the wing give the butterfly lift, like an aircraft's wings.

Each butterfly and moth has its own flight pattern. Wood white butterflies tend to flutter, while purple emperors almost soar. The smaller the butterfly, the faster the wings need to beat to keep the butterfly aloft. Moths tend to fly much faster and straighter than butterflies. Among the fastest is the hawkmoth.

Did you know?

Some moths can fly at up to 30 mph (48 km/h) when they are frightened.

Night watch

There are many, many more moths in the world than there are butterflies. Some are very bright and colorful, especially in the tropics. The Madagascan sunset moth and the Sloane's urania of the Caribbean are as colorful as any butterfly. Closer to home, the moon, or luna, moth with its long tails is quite spectacular. Most moths, though, are drab colored and fly by night. To see them, you have to go out in the backyard at dusk or soon after nightfall. Of course, it is hard to see moths flying in the dark. But because moths fly toward light (see Close-up: Why moths fly to light), you can get them to come to you by making a light frame, as shown in this project.

MAKING A MOTH SCREEN

You will need:

✔ 16 small screws
✔ White cotton cloth
✔ A screwdriver
✔ Thumbtacks
✔ A flashlight
✔ Four small angle brackets
✔ Four lengths of wood, each about 25 inches (60 cm) long

1 With an adult's help, screw a bracket onto one end of each of the lengths of wood. Make sure that the bend of the bracket lines up exactly with the end of the wood.

2 Now join one length of wood to another at right angles by screwing the free end of the bracket into the neighboring length of wood. Do this three more times to make a complete square.

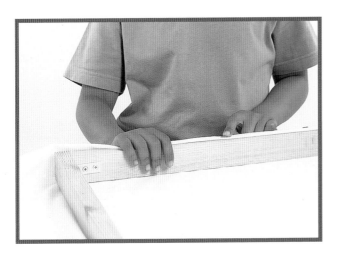

3 Lay the wooden square down on the sheet of white cloth. Make sure the cloth is as flat as possible. Then pull the cloth up tightly over the wood all the way around. Fold it over on top and pin it firmly in place with thumbtacks.

Catching moths
Go out into the backyard with your screen just as it is getting dark. Get a friend to shine a flashlight on the screen from close behind it. After 15 minutes or so, some insects should begin to land on the screen. Many are likely to be moths.

CLOSE-UP *Why moths fly to light*
Scientists do not know exactly why moths fly toward light. They all agree, though, that light does not actually attract moths. One theory is that moths mistake any strong light at night for the moon. The moths are thought to use the moon to steer by. The theory says that moths try to keep the moon in the same place in their view all the time. This works with the moon because it is very far away. A nearby light confuses them. The theory says that the moths spiral in toward the light as they try to keep it in the same place in their view. Few people, however, have seen moths actually spiraling in like this. Another theory is that the sheer brightness of the light gives the moth a blind spot in their eyes which they fly toward.

Butterfly senses

Did you know?
The painted lady is one of the most widespread of all butterflies. It is common almost all over the world.

Butterflies and moths sense the world differently than humans do. They have two eyes like humans, but these eyes are very different from human ones. Butterfly and moth eyes are compound eyes. That means they are made up from hundreds or even thousands of tiny eyelets.

Each eyelet gives a slightly different view, and the butterfly's brain puts them together into one picture. Butterflies and moths are quite nearsighted. But their eyes give an all-around view, and they see many views of the same thing. So they are quick to spot the slight movement of an approaching enemy.

Touching and feeling

Butterflies and moths also have highly sensitive stalks on their heads called feelers, or antennae. Feelers are very useful organs. They are not only used for feeling things. Butterflies and moths can actually hear with them, too, by picking up the vibrations in the air made by sounds.

Butterflies and moths can even taste and smell food with their feelers. In fact, the feelers are so sensitive to smell that butterflies and moths use them to pick up the scent of the flowers they feed on.

Flower detectors
The feelers and feet of a butterfly like this painted lady are highly sensitive organs. They are perfectly adapted to pick up the scent and taste of flowers.

The sensitive feelers can even pick up the scent of a single bloom from hundreds of yards away. The ability of a butterfly's feelers to pick up scents means they play a part in finding a mate, too. Butterflies even use their feelers for smelling out which plants are suitable for laying eggs on.

Besides feelers, a butterfly has another pair of sensory organs on its head—shorter stalks called palps. Like feelers, palps help the butterfly tell which plants are good to lay eggs on. They also help tell the butterfly whether food is good or not.

Butterflies and moths can taste and smell with their feet, or *tarsi*, as well as with their feelers. When you see a butterfly touching a flower with its feet, it is probably trying it for taste.

Did you know?

A male emperor moth can smell a female more than 7 miles (11 km) away, even when the wind is blowing the other way!

Flower power

Adult butterflies and moths do not chew their food. Instead, most suck up liquids through their long hollow tongue, or proboscis, which acts like a drinking straw. Most butterflies and moths drink nectar. Nectar is the sweet liquid made by flowers to attract butterflies and bees, which play a key part in spreading the flowers' pollen.

Fruit and sap feeders

Some woodland butterflies such as red admirals do not feed on flower nectar. Instead, they suck on rotting fruit, or sap that oozes from wounds in trees. Speckled wood butterflies feed on honeydew, the sweet liquid oozed by tiny plant-eating insects called aphids. Many male butterflies also flock down on muddy puddles to suck up dissolved salts. Some even sip animal dung for the nutrients it contains.

Longwing butterflies of the tropics live on pollen as well as nectar. They pick up the pollen in a ring around their proboscis, then moisten it with saliva and swallow it. Pollen helps keep longwings alive for many months. Nectar is not so nourishing. That is why most butterflies live only a few weeks.

Swallowtail butterfly on daisy
The caterpillars of swallowtails feed on plants like parsley, but adults sip nectar from many flowers.

Did you know?
The Darwin's hawkmoth has a proboscis 1 foot (30 cm) long. This is good for sucking nectar from deep, narrow orchids.

Finding food

Butterflies and moths find food flowers by sight, scent, and taste. Because butterflies fly by day, they tend to rely more on sight. Most moths fly at night, and so are drawn to flowers mainly by scent. Each kind of moth or butterfly has a particular range of flowers, or even just a single flower, that it always feeds on (see Butterfly garden, page 17).

Once it finds the right flower, a butterfly or moth uncoils its proboscis and sucks out the nectar. The length of its proboscis often determines which flower it feeds on. The nectar is very deep inside some flowers, such as nasturtiums and many lilies. This means that only a moth with a long proboscis, such as a hawkmoth or sphinx moth, can feed on them.

CLOSE-UP *Close relationships*

Butterflies and moths often have a close relationship with the flowers they feed on. The flowers make nectar that butterflies and moths eat. In return, butterflies and moths spread the flowers' pollen as they flit from flower to flower with pollen stuck on their hairy legs. This two-way relationship is called mutualism. In some cases, this relationship has become very close indeed. A butterfly or moth may rely entirely on one kind of flower for food—and that flower may rely entirely on the insect to pollinate it. Certain kinds of orchid and morning glory flowers, for example, have such deep, narrow blooms that only certain hawkmoths can feed on them. Similarly, yucca plants in the southwestern deserts of the United States are pollinated only by yucca moths—and each kind of yucca plant is pollinated only by a particular kind of yucca moth. Yucca moth caterpillars feed only on yucca fruits. These fruits can only grow once yucca flowers have been pollinated by yucca moths. So neither the moth nor the plant can survive without the other.

Butterfly garden

As farming and other human activity changes the landscape, backyards are becoming important refuges for butterflies. You can help them by creating a butterfly garden in your own backyard. A butterfly garden attracts butterflies so you can observe them closely. A butterfly garden has other benefits, too. Butterflies help flowers multiply by spreading their pollen, filling your backyard with color.

You do not need a backyard to set up a butterfly garden; even a box on a window ledge will attract butterflies. To create the most effective butterfly garden, you need plants that provide food for caterpillars, as well as flower nectar for the adults.

BUTTERFLY GARDEN

You will need:
- ✔ Seeds (or bedding plants) for the right combination of flowers (see right)
- ✔ Potting compost
- ✔ A plant sprayer
- ✔ Plastic cups

1 Buy seeds for the butterflies you wish to attract (see chart at right). Check on the packet that the time of year is right for planting. Then push a few seeds into plastic cups filled with compost.

2 Keep the seed pots in a cool, dark place and water them every day. Soon the first shoots should appear. When they have three or four leaves on them, prepare to transplant them.

3 Decide where you want to plant your garden. Add some compost to the soil and make a small hole with your finger for each plant. Take the seedlings carefully from the seed pots and place them in the hole. Pat soil gently around to hold them in place.

Growing garden
Water the plants regularly, and soon you will have a garden full of plants that will attract butterflies.

CLOSE-UP *Plants to attract butterflies*

GOOD SOURCES OF NECTAR FOR BUTTERFLIES	FLOWERING TIME
SHRUBS	
Azalea	spring
Buddleia	midsummer/fall
Lilac	spring
Privet	spring
ANNUALS	
Alyssum	summer/fall
Marigold	summer/fall
Scabious	summer/fall
Verbena	midsummer/fall
Zinnia	summer/fall
PERENNIALS	
Aster	summer/fall
Daisy	summer
Phlox	summer/fall
Primrose	spring
Purple coneflower	summer
WILDFLOWERS	
Black-eye susan	late summer
Blazing star	summer
Dandelion	spring/fall
Milkweed	summer
New England aster	late summer
Yarrow	early summer

FOOD PLANTS FOR CATERPILLARS	CATERPILLAR
Clover	blues, sulfurs
Elm	mourning cloak
Grasses	satyrs, fiery skipper
Hackberry	hackberry, tawny emperor, snout
Hawthorn	gray hairstreak, banded purple
Mallow	common hairstreak, skipper
Milkweed	monarch
Mustard	whites
Nettle	red admiral, peacock, painted lady, tortoiseshell, comma
Parsley	swallowtails
Plantain	buckeye
Poplar	mourning cloak, white admiral, tiger swallowtail, viceroy
Thistle	painted lady
Violet	fritillary
Wild cherry	coral hairstreak, tiger swallowtail

Finding a mate

Did you know?
Male butterflies mate several times. Females mate just once. Once mated, females give out a scent to deter other males.

A few adult butterflies and moths live several years, but most live only a few weeks. So they have only a short while to find a mate. Females tend to live for only a few days. So they must find a mate and lay their eggs very quickly.

The female usually starts off the mating process. Sometimes even before she has emerged from her pupa (see Life stages, pages 22–23), she sends out scents. These scents, which are called pheromones, are designed to attract males. Male butterflies tend to emerge from their pupae a little earlier than females. The male picks up the female's scent and is sometimes waiting ready nearby. He mates with her as soon she emerges from her pupa.

Scenting a female

Usually, though, the male has to find a female from a distance. Females are detected by sight and by scent. There are scent detectors on the male's feelers especially designed to pick up the scent of a female. Male moths with large feathery feelers, like saturniid moths, can detect a female from many miles away.

Blue male
Male butterflies are often much brighter colored than females. This is the male Karner blue butterfly. The female of the species is mostly drab brown and gray.

Not all male butterflies chase after females. Some stake out territories where they perch and wait for a female to pass by. Nor do all males work alone. Some kinds of male moths gather into swarms to swirl around females. Male European ghost moths form into swarms as the sun goes down, and the females then fly into the swarms.

Once a male and female butterfly or moth find each other, the male begins to court

ON THE TRACK *Butterfly eggs*

Butterfly eggs are very small and are best seen with a magnifying glass. Although the eggs are tiny, you can often find them by watching a female look for a suitable place to lay them. You can also find them by learning which plants the caterpillars feed on, and looking on those.

2. This egg belongs to a cabbage white butterfly. Like the eggs of all yellows and whites, it is shaped like a bottle. You will find cabbage white eggs on cabbages, radishes, and nasturtium flowers.

4. The eggs of the orange tip butterfly are among the easiest of all to spot. They are pale yellow when first laid, but after a few days, turn bright orange. They are laid on garlic mustard.

5. Like peacocks, the red admiral lays its eggs singly on the upper side of nettle leaves. The eggs look just like little golf balls.

1. Swallowtail butterflies lay large, smooth, round, brown eggs. Each kind of swallowtail has its own favorite plant. Black swallowtails like parsley and carrot.

3. Peacocks lay their eggs on nettle leaves. But peacock eggs are laid not singly, but in big clusters, hidden on the underside of the leaves.

the female. The bright colors of a male butterfly's wings may play a part in attracting a female. So, too, may scents released by scales on the male's wings called androconia. Indeed, a male will often rub his wings over a female's feelers to let her smell this scent.

The courting pattern varies from species to species. Occasionally, the courtship is very elaborate. The male may dance a fluttering dance around the female, or bump into her. The two of them land gently on a plant and stroke each other with their feelers. Eventually, they mate, and the female looks for a site to lay her eggs.

Did you know?
While mating, butterflies stay on a plant or the ground. But if danger threatens, they fly off linked together.

Eggs and caterpillars

Butterflies and moths begin life as eggs. After mating, a few female butterflies just scatter their eggs on the ground. But most find a place where they know the caterpillars will find food when they hatch out. Each kind of caterpillar has its own favorite food plant. So using her sensitive feelers, the female butterfly seeks out the right plant. She then stamps or scratches the plant with her feet to make sure the plant is right—and that no other butterfly has been there before. Then she lays eggs singly or in clusters up to a thousand. This project shows how you can hatch butterfly eggs and then look after the caterpillars as they grow.

HATCHING EGGS

You will need:

✔ Butterfly eggs on their food plant. You may find these yourself, but it is better to get them from a reputable supplier (see page 31).

✔ Plentiful supplies of the caterpillars' food plant (see page 17)

✔ A plant sprayer

✔ A plastic food container
✔ A large screw top jar
✔ Light netting material
✔ Tape and a craft knife
✔ Protective gloves

1 Put a little water in a screw top jar. Then, using gloves, place the plant with eggs on into the jar. Screw on the lid. Then watch the eggs frequently over the next week or so.

2 When you see signs of change in the eggs, transfer them and their food plant to a dry food container. When the caterpillars hatch, put a lid on the container to keep them from escaping.

3 Keep your caterpillars well supplied with the leaves of their food plant. You will soon see them grow in stages, called instars. After a few days, they will need air, so ask an adult to cut a window in the lid of the container. Then tape netting over this to keep the caterpillars from escaping.

ON THE TRACK *Caterpillars*

There are far more caterpillars than there are adult butterflies and moths, but most are eaten or killed by disease. You can often find them on the plants they choose as food.

3

3. The monarch caterpillar feeds only on milkweed. Milkweed makes the caterpillar poisonous for birds to eat.

1

1. Red admiral caterpillars live on nettle leaves. As they eat, they use leaves to build tents around themselves. This hides them until they are full grown.

4

4. Silver spotted skipper caterpillars grow 2 inches (5 cm) long and feed on sheep's fescue plants.

2. Cabbage white butterfly caterpillars are small and green. As their name suggests, they feed on plants like cabbages.

5. Swallowtail caterpillars feed on fennel, wild carrot, angelica, rue, and milk parsley. They emit a foul smell when threatened.

2

5

Catching butterflies

Put the lid with the window back on the container. Keep the caterpillars well supplied with the right leaves, and give them a very light sprinkle of water every day or so. Do not put water in the container to keep the leaves fresh; the caterpillars will become bloated. Watch the caterpillars as they grow steadily bigger over about a week, depending on the kind.

Life stages

Caterpillars are eating machines. Many can eat several times their own body weight in a day. After a few weeks, eating and growing, the caterpillar is ready to become a pupa, or chrysalis. This is the stage in its life when it changes into an adult butterfly or moth. The caterpillar's skin forms a casing, and the caterpillar changes to an adult inside. Many moth caterpillars spin a silken case or cocoon around the pupa for protection. Others tunnel underground, or make a case of leaves. Butterfly pupa rely on camouflage or lying hidden under dead leaves. Pupa look lifeless. This project shows how you can watch adults emerge from pupa.

EMERGING BUTTERFLIES

You will need:

- ✔ Butterfly caterpillars from a supplier (see page 31) or from eggs that you hatch yourself (see pages 20–21).
- ✔ A plant sprayer
- ✔ A plastic food container
- ✔ Light netting material
- ✔ Tape and a craft knife
- ✔ Protective gloves
- ✔ A large laundry bag

CLOSE-UP *Monarch life cycle*

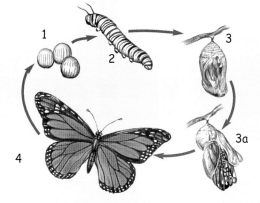

Like all butterflies, the monarch goes through four main stages in its life. It begins life as an egg (1), then hatches into a larva or caterpillar (2). When it is big enough, the caterpillar turns into a pupa (3). Inside the pupa case, the caterpillar metamorphoses (changes) into an adult butterfly. When ready, it breaks out (3a) and flies away (4).

1 Put the caterpillars in a container with a netting window, as shown on page 21. When ready to become pupae, the caterpillars crawl up to hang upside down from the lid on a silken thread. They then curl up in J-shape to form the casing.

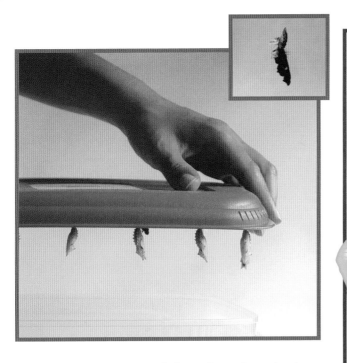

ON THE TRACK *Butterfly pupae*

Butterfly pupae may be seen hanging upside down from a silken thread. They also hang out from stems, or lie on or in the ground, but these are hard to spot.

1. Monarch pupae look like tiny, green jade vases at first. When the adult is about to emerge, the casing becomes more and more transparent.

1

2

2. Orange tips spend 10 months as pupae, hanging out from a stem. But they are very rarely seen in the wild.

3

3. Great spangled fritillary pupae hang down from branches near clumps of violets.

4. Mourning cloak caterpillars often feed on willows, but the pupae often form on other trees. Adults emerge in late summer.

4

5

5. Swallowtails hang out from stems, supported by a silken thread around the middle.

2 Lift the lid very carefully and gently to check the pupae regularly. Spray them lightly with water once a day, or more often in hot weather. Eventually, you should see the pupae darkening in color. That means they are about to emerge.

Newly emerged butterflies

The adult butterflies emerge from the pupa after 7–14 days, usually in mid-morning. Leave them for 3–4 hours so the wings can inflate and dry out, or overnight if the adults emerge in the afternoon. It is then best to set them free. But if you want to observe them for a few days first, release them from the container into a large laundry bag. Place a sponge saturated with a mix of 20 percent honey and 80 percent water in a dish in the bag every day. Set them free after three days, preferably on a sunny day.

You can handle most butterflies if you are very, very careful and gentle. Hold them lightly in cupped hands, taking care not to crush the wings.

The battle for survival

Did you know?
Puss moth caterpillars can squirt a jet of harmful acid if threatened with attack.

Both adult butterflies and moths, and their caterpillars, have many enemies. They are preyed upon by birds, bats, lizards, spiders, hornets, beetles, and many other creatures.

Butterflies and moths have a number of ways to protect themselves from attack. Many butterflies and moths hide from their enemies by taking on the colors and patterns of trees, leaves, and rocks. This is called camouflage. It is especially important for moths, since they rest during the day. This is why they are mostly drab colors. The wings of many moths blend in perfectly with the tree trunks or dead leaves where they rest.

Butterflies fold their brightly colored wings together to avoid being seen so easily. The tops of the brimstone butterfly's wings

CLOSE-UP *Caterpillar defenses*

Caterpillars are especially vulnerable to attack since they cannot fly away. Many caterpillars are colored green and look like leaves and grass. Brown ones look like mud and bark. Others have two bright spots on their bodies that look like eyes. So they look just like a poisonous snake, not a harmless caterpillar. Many caterpillars, though, are genuinely dangerous. They have developed chemicals that make them poisonous to attackers, or at least make them smell or taste bad. Swallowtail caterpillars emit a foul smell when threatened. Browntail moth caterpillars have hairs tipped with poison that can give people a rash. Spurge hawkmoth caterpillars and many others are also poisonous. But poison will only save a caterpillar if an attacker knows they are poisonous. So poisonous caterpillars are usually brightly colored to warn enemies off.

The monarch butterfly caterpillar feeds on milkweed, which contains a powerful poison. This makes the caterpillar itself poisonous.

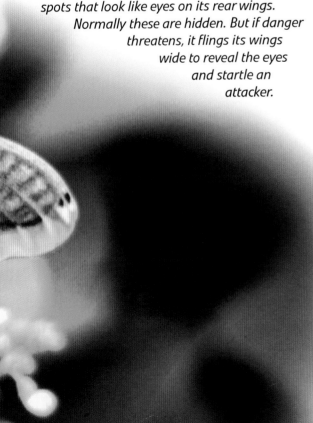

Polyphemus moth
Like many moths, the polyphemus has big spots that look like eyes on its rear wings. Normally these are hidden. But if danger threatens, it flings its wings wide to reveal the eyes and startle an attacker.

are bright yellow, but the undersides are green. When the brimstone butterfly folds its wings up to rest, it looks just like the green leaf of a tree.

Decoys and flashing eyes

Camouflage works while butterflies and moths are resting, but if they move, they become visible. So butterflies and moths that fly by day may adopt other strategies.

Some mimic dangerous creatures. The hornet clearwing moth looks just like a stinging wasp. Others have wing shapes and colors designed to confuse. Some have false heads and feelers on their wingtips so that birds attack the wrong end. Others, like eyed hawkmoths, have bright patches on their rear wings that look just like giant eyes. When in danger, the moth startles its enemy by flinging the wings wide to reveal these big eyes.

Butterflies on the move

Butterflies and moths depend entirely on outside warmth. They even need to bask in the sun for a while to gain enough energy to fly off. In winter, they have real problems moving. In winter, too, the vegetation that they depend on dies off. So butterflies and moths that spend the winter in cold places become inactive. They go into a state called diapause, in which their body processes all but stop.

Winter life stages

Different butterflies and moths enter their winter diapause at different stages in their lives. Some pass the winter as eggs. Others spend it as caterpillars. They build up chemicals in their bodies that prevent them from freezing when the weather turns really cold. Some butterflies and moths get through the winter as pupae. A few, like tortoiseshell butterflies and underwing moths, sleep through the winter as adults. They hide in a hollow tree or under bark. They even fly about on warmer days in the winter. They are often the first butterflies to appear in the spring.

Did you know?

Oleander hawkmoths are perhaps the greatest long distance fliers. They can fly fast and far over huge distances.

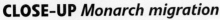

CLOSE-UP *Monarch migration*

The most famous migrating butterflies of all are the monarchs of North America. Every fall, huge swarms gather to fly south to the Mexican mountains or the California coast. Some individual butterflies may fly 2,000 miles (3,000 km) on this journey. In spring, the monarchs mate, and fly north again. The females lay their eggs on the way. Most of the adults die along the way. But the eggs hatch, and the butterflies that eventually emerge continue the journey northward.

Moving away

A few species of butterfly move away, or migrate, when times are hard. Some migrate to find a warmer climate. Some migrate to find new plant growth. Some migrate simply to get away from overpopulated areas.

Butterflies are strong fliers and can travel long distances. Painted lady butterflies, for instance, spend the winter in tropical North Africa and Mexico. When spring comes around, they fly all the way north to cooler regions in Europe and the United States.

Some butterflies are worldwide travelers. Occasionally, small swarms of North American butterflies are seen in Europe after flying over the Atlantic. Crimson speckled moths have been seen far out over the South Atlantic Ocean.

Unlike birds, however, butterflies rarely make a round trip. Usually an adult will make the journey one way, but only its offspring will make the journey back. Some butterflies even go through several generations on the way. The amazing thing is that the grandchildren seem to know where to go back to, even though they have never been there before.

Monarch feeding

In summer, the monarch feeds on milkweed in North America. As fall nears, it begins its long flight south.

Identifying butterflies

Scientists group butterflies and moths into 24 superfamilies. Only two superfamilies are butterflies: the Papilionoidea and the Hesperioidea. The other 22 are all moths. Start to identify a butterfly by placing it in a family as shown here. Use the wing shapes as a guide.

PAPILIONOIDEA, OR TRUE BUTTERFLY, FAMILIES

SWALLOWTAILS: Known scientifically as *Papilionidae*.

WHITES AND YELLOWS: Known scientifically as *Pieridae*.

HAIRSTREAKS, COPPERS, AND BLUES: Known scientifically as *Lycaenidae*.

MONARCHS AND METALMARKS: Known scientifically as *Danainae* and *Riodiniadae*.

ADMIRALS, TORTOISESHELLS, FRITILLARIES: Known scientifically as *Nymphalidae*.

BROWNS: Known scientifically as *Satyrinae*.

THE HESPERIOIDEA, OR SKIPPER, SUPERFAMILY

SKIPPERS: Known scientifically as *Hesperidae*.

SOME MOTH SUPERFAMILIES

ROYAL MOTHS: Known scientifically as *Saturniidae*.

HAWKMOTHS: Known scientifically as *Sphingidae*.

TIGER MOTHS: Known scientifically as *Arctiidae*.

SWALLOWTAILS

This family includes tropical birdwings, the biggest of all butterflies.

Distinguishing features:
• Medium to big butterflies. Big over-lapping wings that are long from front to back.

Swallowtails: Subfamily PAPLIONINAE
Swallowtails have long tails on their hindwings. They fly and glide well. Many are protected from birds by mimicking the color of bad tasting butterflies.
Swallowtails include: *Tiger swallowtails*

Apollos, festoons: Subfamily PARNASSIINAE, ZERYNTHIAE
Unlike true swallowtails, apollos have no wing tails, and flap heavily when flying. Unusually for butterflies, they make their pupae in cocoonlike webs among leaves on the ground.
Apollos include: *Clouded apollos, parnassians*

WHITES AND YELLOWS

A large family of light, brightly colored, medium-sized butterflies.

Distinguishing features:
• Distinctive pale yellow and white color with small, straight-edged wings.

Whites and orange tips: Subfamily PIERINAE
Most whites have black wings; orange tips have orange wingtips. Some whites, like cabbage whites, are disliked by gardeners because the caterpillars eat leaves voraciously.
Whites include: *Cabbage whites, wood whites*

Yellows and brimstones: Subfamily COLIADINAE
Yellow butterflies are also known as sulfurs, because they are a dull yellow color like powdered sulfur. Brimstones are among the longest lived butterflies, living almost a year.
Yellows include: *Clouded yellows, orange sulfurs*

HAIRSTREAKS, BLUES, AND COPPERS

This family includes little blues, some of the smallest of all butterflies.

Distinguishing feature:
• Many have lacy wings in shimmering colors.

Hairstreak (gossamer winged): Subfamily THECLINAE
Hairstreaks get their name from the pale, hairlike streaks under their wings. The wings are usually held folded up and often have short tails.
Hairstreaks include: *Grays, great purples*

Blues and coppers: Subfamily POLYOMMATINAE
Blues are named for the shimmering blue upper side of most males. Some males and most female blues are actually brown. Coppers are bright orange or copper, often with black spots.
Blues, coppers include: *Small copper, spring azure*

MONARCHS AND METALMARKS

Monarchs live in North America, metalmarks mostly in tropical Latin America.

Distinguishing features:
• Monarchs have black-veined orange wings.
• Metalmarks have metallic wing markings.

Monarchs: Subfamily DANAINAE
Monarchs have a strong flapping, gliding flight. They are famed for their annual migration from North America to Mexico. Monarch caterpillars taste so bad that birds will not eat them.
Monarchs include: *Monarchs, plain tigers*

Metalmarks: Subfamily RIODINIADAE
Metalmarks are small butterflies. They are hard to recognize, because many have colors and wing shapes that mimic other bad-tasting butterflies.
Metalmarks include: *Duke of Burgundys*

ADMIRALS, TORTOISESHELLS, FRITILLARIES

Often called the brush-foots, this is the biggest of all the families of butterflies.

Distinguishing features:
• Short front legs covered in brushlike tufts.
• Wings often have toothlike edge markings.

Admirals, emperors: Subfamily LIMENITIDINAE, APATURINAE
These large, colorful butterflies have dark brown or black upper sides crossed by a white band. Many live in woodlands and feed on tree sap.
Admirals include: *Purple emperors, white admirals*

Tortoiseshells and others: Subfamily VANESSIDINAE
The wings of these large, fast-flying butterflies, called the vanessids, often have jagged edges.
Vanessids include: *Mourning cloaks, painted ladies, peacocks, commas, red admirals*

Fritillaries and longwings: Subfamily HELICONIINAE
Fritillary is another word for spotted, and the wings of these butterflies are covered in black spots. They are also known as checkerspots. Scientists called them heliconids.
Heliconids include: *Zebras, gulf fritillaries*

BROWNS

This small family of dark brown or orange butterflies are also known as satyrs.

Distinguishing feature:
• Wings usually have small, eyelike spots.

Marbled whites and graylings: Subfamily SATYRINAE
These small butterflies are usually plentiful in woods and on grassland in the summer. Their eyespots may help protect them from birds that might otherwise eat them.
Satyrs include: *Red satyrs, pearly eyes*

SKIPPERS

Skippers are small butterflies that have bodies shaped like moths but they fly by day.

Distinguishing features:
- Fast, skipping, darting flight.
- Narrow, sharply angled wings.

Grizzled skippers: Subfamily PYRGINAE
Grizzled, or spread-wing, skippers are usually sooty brown with white spots. Grizzled means spotty. Like moths, their wings have a furry appearance.
Grizzled skippers include: *Silver-spotted skippers, long-tailed skippers, cloudywings*

Golden, or grass, skippers: Subfamily HESPERIINAE
Golden skippers are a brown or gold color. They bask with hindwings flat and forewings raised.
Golden skippers include: *Fiery skippers, orange skipperlings, sunrise skippers*

HAWKMOTHS

This is a family of large, very fast-flying moths, also known as sphinx moths.

Distinguishing features:
- Big bodies and long, swept back wings.

Hummingbird moths
Many hawkmoths fly by day. They look like hummingbirds as they hover in front of flowers sipping the flowers' nectar. So they are called hummingbird moths. Many have clear wings with no scales, so are called clearwing moths.
Hummingbird moths include: *Hummingbird moths, bumblebee moths, white-lined sphinx moths*

Hornworm moths
The caterpillars of many hawkmoths have a hornlike point at the rear, so they are called hornworms.
Hornworm moths include: *Tomato hornworms*

ROYAL MOTHS

This huge superfamily includes some of the largest and most spectacular moths.

Distinguishing features:
- Large wings and vivid colors.

Moon moths
Moon, or luna, moths are large, spectacular moths with long wingtails like crescent moons. They have soft white or pale gold fur on their bodies.
Moon moths: *American luna moths, Indian moon moths*

Other royal moths
The royal moths or Saturniids are also known as giant silk moths. They are called silk moths because their caterpillars spin themselves big silk cocoons when they pupate.
Royal moths include: *Cecropia moths, polyphemus moths, io moths, imperial moths, promethea moths*

TIGER MOTHS

Tiger moths are small to medium sized moths with narrow wings.

Distinguishing features:
- Black and yellow or black and red stripes on their bodies.

Tiger moths
Many tiger moths have bright colored patterns on their wings. This helps protect the moths, because the bright colors suggest to a hunting bird that they might be distasteful.
Tiger moths include: *Garden tigers, leopard moths*

Woolly bears (caterpillars)
The caterpillars of many tiger moths are covered in thick fur and are called woolly bears. They are often seen in fall after they leave their food plants and search for a place to sleep out the winter.
Woolly bears include: *Yellow bears, woolly bears*

Glossary

abdomen Rear part of a butterfly, moth, or other insect's body. It holds the digestive system, the heart and breathing system, and the reproductive system.

annual A plant that grows from seed, flowers and dies in a single year.

antenna (plural **antennae**) Long, thin sense organ on an insect's head, sometimes known as feeler. It responds to smell, taste, and touch.

camouflage Colors and patterns used by a butterfly, moth, or other animal to help it blend into the background and not be seen.

caterpillar The larva of a butterfly or moth. It has a long, soft body and many short legs.

chrysalis A pupa, the stage in a butterfly's life when it changes from a caterpillar to an adult.

cocoon A protective silk bag that a caterpillar creates before it becomes a chrysalis.

compound eye One of an insect's eyes, made up from many tiny eyelets.

exoskeleton The hard protective outer casing of an insect's body that provides all its support.

iridescence Shimmering, rainbow colors that seem to shift and change when they are seen from different angles.

larva (plural **larvae**) The young stage in a butterfly, moth, or other insect's life before it undergoes complete metamorphosis to become an adult.

lepidoptera The scientific name for all butterflies and moths.

metamorphosis The transformation of a young butterfly, moth, or other insect into an adult in a series of stages.

migration An animal's long seasonal journey to find food or to breed.

mutualism Relationship between two living things in which each helps the other.

nectar Sweet liquid made by flowers to attract insects so that they help spread flower pollen.

palps A pair of short sense organs at the front of a butterfly or moth's head.

perennial Plant that flowers year after year.

pheromone Body part with particular function, such as the heart or liver.

proboscis Tubelike mouthparts of insects that suck liquid foods.

pupa (plural **pupae**) Stage before a butterfly, moth, or other insect becomes an adult.

scales The tiny plates that cover the wings of a butterfly or moth.

thorax The middle section of an insect's body where the wings and legs are attached.

tympanal membrane Thin skin stretched over the tympanal organs.

tympanal organs Cavities in a moth's thorax that act like ears.

FURTHER READING:
David Carter. Eyewitness Handbooks *Butterflies and Moths*. New York, NY: Dorling Kindersley, 1992.
Richard Walton. National Audubon *Pocket Guide to Familiar Butterflies of North America*. Pleasantville, MA: Alfred A. Knopf, 1990.

FIND OUT ABOUT REARING BUTTERFLIES:
Monarch Watch
http://www.monarchwatch.org

Index